Original title:
The Meaning of Life: Still Under Investigation

Copyright © 2025 Creative Arts Management OÜ
All rights reserved.

Author: Zachary Prescott
ISBN HARDBACK: 978-1-80566-147-4
ISBN PAPERBACK: 978-1-80566-442-0

Whispers of Existence

In the fridge lies my purpose,
Some leftovers from last week,
They whisper sweet existence,
But who knows if they speak?

The cat thinks it's a joke,
Chasing shadows all day long,
As I ponder in my cloak,
Is this where I belong?

I tried to ask the goldfish,
For wisdom in its bowl,
It just swam in circles,
Ignoring my deep soul.

Between naps and snacks I roam,
Seeking enlightenment anew,
Guess I'll just stay home,
Until someone brings the stew.

Echoes in the Cosmos

Underneath the starry skies,
I ponder with a snack in hand,
Do aliens know our highs?
Or just our fries from fast food land?

With each twinkling little star,
I try to decode the blips,
But all I find from afar,
Are potato chip and dip scripts.

The moon's winking at our plight,
As I struggle for my dreams,
Maybe I'll shine tonight,
Or burst at the seams, it seems.

So here's to questions unasked,
To laughter and cosmic fun,
Life's one big goofy task,
In this game that's never done.

Threads of Time and Thought

Time's a sweater with loose seams,
Each thread pulled can lead me astray,
I wonder if it's a series of dreams,
Or just laundry day, hey hey!

As I untangle this mess of clues,
My dog barks at the passing moon,
Was I supposed to wear these shoes?
Or is the day ending too soon?

With silly thoughts and goofy minds,
I chase the ticking clock's tick,
Finding wisdom in what unwinds,
Would it be easier if I were a brick?

As the sun sets with a grin,
I ponder my fluffy fate,
Maybe tomorrow I'll begin,
With coffee and only a bit of cake.

Searching for Stars in the Mundane

The coffee spills, it's a sign,
That blessings hide in muck and grind,
I sip and search for the divine,
In every drop that fate designed.

In socks that don't match, I find laughter,
The laundry is my cosmic quest,
Perhaps joy is in the hereafter,
Or just in finding out who's best.

With the laundry basket as my throne,
I ponder what it's all about,
Yet comfort's found when I'm alone,
In my spaceship of socks, no doubt.

So here's to the wacky grind,
In the mess, I might just spark,
A joy that's sweet and so aligned,
As I traverse the cosmic park.

Melodies from the Invisible

A tune plays softly, no one to hear,
Chasing shadows, hinting at cheer.
I dance with my coffee, it spills on the floor,
A symphony crafted, yet no encore.

Invisible whispers, a cosmic joke,
Where laughter and giggles are all that provoke.
I sing with the stars, in pajamas so bright,
While pondering snacks as my greatest delight.

Canvas of a Restless Mind

Painting the thoughts that bounce all around,
With colors of chaos, in laughter they're found.
A brush made of whimsy, strokes soft and wide,
Crafting dreams that giggle, in playful divide.

Doodles of worries, all scribbled in jest,
A canvas that's messy is truly the best.
Crayons of comfort, they melt in the sun,
Art that makes sense, or sense that is fun?

Phantoms of the Heart

Ghosts of my feelings, they waltz on the floor,
In awkward spin circles, who knows what's in store?
They trip on their capes, at the shiver of night,
A love that's amusing, a comical fright.

Boo! said the silence, with a wink and a grin,
As I search for my socks, my adventure begins.
In echoing laughter, I chase what I seek,
These phantoms of joy make my heart feel unique.

Dances in the Unseen

Unseen partners sway in a phantom parade,
With twinkling shoes that no sunlight has made.
I join in the frolic, all giggles and cheer,
In this secret soirée, where nonsense runs near.

Each step is a riddle, each twirl is a jest,
As balloons filled with laughter invite me to rest.
In shadows we shimmy, where fun takes the lead,
With dance moves that wiggle, the heart finds its creed.

Untold Stories of the Ordinary

In shadows of the mundane day,
A lost sock dreams of grandeur play.
The cat's the king, with no job to do,
While we toil in jobs, for bosses so blue.

The neighbor's lawn grows bright and green,
While ours looks like a desert scene.
Yet still we smile, as life rolls along,
In this wacky world, we all belong.

Puzzles Beyond Perception

Why do donuts have holes, I ask?
It's a culinary, puzzling task.
And socks mysteriously vanish too,
Is there a portal? Does it sound true?

The fridge hums softly, a tune so sweet,
It holds our secrets, our late-night treat.
Yet every morning, we find the same,
Leftover pizza, it's always the same.

Reflections in the Glass of Time

A mirror shows the face we know,
But hides the puns life likes to throw.
It laughs at wrinkles, it jokes at our hair,
As time whispers softly, "No one's aware."

Tick-tock, the clock goes on its spree,
Life's little quirks, oh, can't you see?
Each second ticks with a giggle and grin,
Like the time you forgot—was it out or in?

A Quest for Glimmers of Truth

We seek truth in cereal boxes at dawn,
Searching for wisdom while munching on,
The mysteries of milk, really sublime,
As clowns juggle donuts—a plasma mime.

In the park, we chase shadows and dreams,
With ice cream in hand, or so it seems.
The universe chuckles, with stars all aglow,
As we wander and wonder, just who do we know?

Reflections on the Brink

Why are we here, just to eat pie?
Are we players on stage or just passing by?
Is existence a riddle with laughter entwined?
Or a cosmic joke left by fate not so kind?

Shoes without laces just flopping around,
Questions like bubbles, they float and they drown.
Do we tap dance on dreams, or tickle the void?
Maybe life's just a gift that's far too toyed!

In Search of Shimmering Truths

I sought for the answers behind all the doors,
But all that I found were some socks and some chores.
The universe chuckles, it spins and it sways,
As I trip on my thoughts in a comical haze.

Each wisdom I grasp slips just out of reach,
A lesson in laughter, the best way to teach.
Do fish ponder currents while munching on fries?
Or do clouds just float by, with their heads in the skies?

A Tapestry of Wondering

In moments of ponder, I scratch at my chin,
Wondering if I'm a loser or winner within.
Do squirrels hold conventions discussing their days?
Or are they just nutty in their furry displays?

I chase after meaning like a cat with a string,
Only to trip over what laughter can bring.
A snap of a twig, and the thought is now gone,
Life's just a sitcom; where do we log on?

Ephemeral Signposts

Oh look, there's a signpost that points to a dream,
But all that I see is a bright purple gleam.
Each path that I take seems to twist and to shout,
While squirrels hold their meetings and critters pout out.

I'm a tourist in life with a map made of fluff,
Searching for meaning, but it's just never enough!
The cosmic guidebook seems lost on the shelf,
Saying, 'Just hang on, and enjoy being yourself.'

Horizons of Hope and Question

Under skies of bright confusion,
We chase dreams with wild precision.
Each clue's a wink, each laugh a sigh,
What's up with us? Oh, who can cry?

We ponder deep, but drink our tea,
And wonder what we're meant to be.
The universe giggles at our plight,
As we dance in circles, just for spite.

Balancing thoughts on wobbly chairs,
While missing socks? Who truly cares?
Life's a riddle wrapped in a jest,
But we'll ace the exam—why not, we jest!

So let's toast to what we can't yet know,
With cupcakes and sprinkles in tow.
For every question leads somewhere bright,
Even if it's just a cupcake bite.

Beyond Certainty's Veil

Underneath a starry haze,
We tumble through our quirky maze.
Answers hide like socks in drawers,
While laughter echoes and hope explores.

With faces scrunched and pencils poised,
We dive into thoughts: can we rejoice?
A dog barks loud in the dense night air,
What's real? Who knows! It's a fun affair.

Here's a theory, let's not forget,
That life's a stage and we're the duet.
Each stumble brings a giggling cheer,
So bring on the chaos, let laughter steer.

In the end, we'll draw a chart,
With squiggly lines and a tip to start.
Guessing wildly at why we roam,
It's all a comedy—welcome home!

Waking Dreams and Silent Screams

A snore, a leap, as morning cheer,
We wake with dreams, yet still adhere.
Mismatched socks and coffee spills,
Ensure our quest for wisdom thrills.

Between sips of joy, we recount the night,
When moonbeams danced and stars took flight.
The meaning's fuzzy, like an old TV,
With static thoughts—what could it be?

In a world of quirks, both big and small,
We question it all, or not at all.
But laughter's balm, we find, not dread,
As we compile our thoughts, still half-baked bread.

Yet in the chaos, there's a spark,
Igniting wonder even in the dark.
So let's embrace this joyful spree,
For life's a riddle—come laugh with me!

Flickers of Insight

In the morning light, I sip my brew,
Wondering why socks vanish, too.
Is there a secret in the dark?
Or just an old cat with a peculiar spark?

I ponder if coding is life's true test,
But can't find the hex code for time's jest.
Life's like a puzzle, missing a piece,
Could it be hiding with my last fleece?

A dance of confusion swirls in my head,
Is it wisdom or just something I've read?
With each new question, I laugh out loud,
Why are we serious? Let's be weirdly proud!

So let's toast to chaos, to unplanned fun,
To figuring out, as we run and run.
Maybe the answer is somewhere near,
In laughter and joy, my heart finds cheer.

Drifting Through the Unknowns

Like a balloon lost in the sky,
I float through thoughts as clouds pass by.
What's the point of this wobbly ride?
Maybe I'll discover it, just on the side.

A squirrel in the yard gives me a grin,
As I ponder where the socks have been.
Do they party in space, or do they roam?
Finding the missing, I'll bring them home.

Each question marks like an unwanted guest,
Why does time always feel like a jest?
With giggles and berries, I fill up my jar,
Life's little mysteries are the best by far.

I'll bounce through the cosmos, float on a breeze,
Unraveling puzzles like a fun mystery tease.
With each silly thought, I cheer and I smile,
Maybe this journey is just worthwhile.

Unveiling the Layers of Being

Peeling back layers like an onion, I see,
Why do we rush and then sip our tea?
Am I a philosopher or just a clown?
In my thoughts, I go up and down.

Between stumbles and trails of crumbs,
A cookie for thought, oh the joy that comes!
Why does wisdom come with a goofy face?
Maybe life's a joke, an adventurous race.

A twist here, a turn there, life's got flair,
Like a cat in a hat, with nibbled hair.
What's it all about, this curious game?
Could it just be a wild, wacky claim?

With giggles and hiccups, I dance through the strife,
Finding sheer joy in this riddle of life.
Let's pull back the curtains and let out a cheer,
Every layer reveals more laughter, my dear.

An Atlas of Inner Landscapes

Mapping my thoughts, it's a wild ride,
Through jungles of questions, where answers hide.
With a compass that spins, I'm lost in the fun,
Hunting for treasures, my search has begun.

Mountains of doubt and rivers of glee,
I scale them with joy, feeling so free.
Do I follow the path, or wander astray?
Perhaps I'll just nap till noontime today.

With every new turn, there's laughter abound,
In this vast inner land, surprises are found.
Is the map just a myth, or is it a game?
Each twist and each turn gives life a new name.

So let's cheer for the journeys, both strange and absurd,
Each misstep a dance, each silence a word.
In the atlas of being, we'll sketch 'til we drop,
Finding humor in chaos, we'll never stop.

In Pursuit of Purpose

I searched for answers in a shoe,
But all I found was an old gum too.
A squirrel laughed from the nearby tree,
Saying, "Life's a joke, just wait and see!"

I tried to ponder as I ate a pie,
Yet the crust whispered, "Just kiss the sky!"
I asked my cat, but he just purred,
And now I'm stuck with my dreams unheard.

The clock ticks loud, but what does it mean?
A waxed-up floor? A movie scene?
I dance on answers that slip and slide,
And wear my doubts like a clownish guide.

No epiphanies in the fridge, oh dear,
Just a moldy cheese, my biggest fear.
But laughter's the key, or so they say,
So I chuckle and wiggle my woes away.

Fragments of Cosmic Clarity

Under starlit skies, I telescope,
To find some wisdom with hopes and hope.
A comet zoomed, left glittering trails,
But all I got were a million emails.

A wise old owl gave me a wink,
Said, "Life's not just a caffeinated drink."
With each sip brewed in cosmic brew,
I spilled some thoughts, and yes, made a stew.

I tossed my worries like confetti bright,
To see them dance in the moonlit light.
A frog croaked loudly, "What's the score?"
A life of questions we all adore.

So here's to puzzles both big and small,
With hiccups and laughter, we'll conquer all.
For clarity comes not in neat little lines,
But in messy moments wrapped in vines.

Beneath the Surface of Being

I dove deep down into my brain,
Searching for gold, but found some rain.
Tickled by thoughts that splashed and flopped,
Like fish on land, I felt quite dropped.

Bubbles of wisdom popped with flair,
While my pet goldfish just gave a stare.
"Look deeper!" they said, "It's not that tough,"
But who knew, pondering could be so rough?

The couch I sat on had many tales,
Of potato chips and wild snail trails.
In the cushions, I found lost socks,
And pondered if truth wears mismatched frocks.

So here I drift in my ocean dream,
Fishing for meaning with a plastic beam.
Embracing the weird, with chuckles around,
In life's swirling depths, joy can be found.

The Quest for Hidden Truths

With a map made of candy, I set off fast,
In search of the truths that speak and blast.
A gopher poked his head, said with a grin,
"Truth's in the pie, let the fun begin!"

I plopped down under a candy cane tree,
Nibbling on truths served bright and free.
Each bite revealed secrets oh so sweet,
But soon I learned they're just tweets in repeat.

The clouds giggled as they changed their shape,
Transforming doubts into a playful cape.
With every whisper of wind and sense,
I juggled my worries like a big circus fence.

So here I am, on this crazy quest,
With laughter and snacks, I feel so blessed.
For sometimes truths are just silly games,
And seeking them out is what fuels the flames.

Fables from the Edge of Reason

Once a cat claimed it could fly,
With wings made of butter, oh my!
It leaped from the wall,
And gave quite a fall.

A wise old dog raised a brow,
"Despite your dream, here and now,
Stay grounded, dear friend,
Or you may just offend."

The fish in the bowl gave a wink,
"Life's not just goldfish and drink!
Complain if you must,
But find joy, that's a must!"

So, laughter was heard in the park,
As squirrels debated the spark,
Of life, as it seems,
Is built on our dreams.

When Life Plays Hide-and-Seek

Life's dancing, a game of charades,
It hides behind bushes and shades.
"Come find me!" it shouts,
While we chase our doubts.

The toaster is laughing, it seems,
As we brew our wildest of dreams.
"I'm right here! Can't you see?"
The kettle agrees with glee.

A sock shouts, "I'm lost! Count to ten!"
While the cat claws the drapes, like a hen.
Life plays its tricks,
With absurd, slippery flicks.

And just when we think we are wise,
Life smiles with all its surprise.
So we dance in a jig,
And embrace our next big gig.

An Odyssey in the Ordinary

There once was a spoon with great dreams,
It longed to be part of grand themes.
But all it could do,
Was stir up the stew.

The fork looked on with a sigh,
"Together, we serve a pie high!
Stop dreaming, let's dine,
And life will be fine!"

A plate said, "Join in the fun!"
"We're more than utensils, my pun!"
With laughter so bright,
They cooked up delight.

An odyssey starts with a meal,
Where friendship and laughter reveal.
In the kitchen we find,
Life's not that unkind.

Labels on Fleeting Moments

Here's a label; it says, "Be Bold!"
As ice cream melts, stories unfold.
With sprinkles and cheer,
The flavors are here.

A moment captured in a jar,
With fireflies, oh, how they spar!
"Don't blink," says the breeze,
"Life's fun if you tease."

A label marked "Do Not Disturb,"
For giggles and silly suburb.
In chaos, we find,
A treasure to bind.

So wrap up your joy with some flair,
And carry it close, everywhere.
For labels may fade,
But laughter won't trade.

Fables of Forgotten Echoes

In a land where wisdom sleeps,
The sheep debate while the farmer leaps.
Chasing shadows, they ponder the skies,
As stars giggle in clever disguise.

A turtle claims to hold the key,
But trips on truths, oh so free.
The rabbits laugh as they hop along,
For in their hearts, they know they're wrong.

With acorns weighed in a ticking clock,
The squirrels ponder their ticking stock.
Chasing leaves and thumping chests,
They yell, 'Who cares? Let's just jest!'

Then a wise old owl with a crooked nose,
Says, 'Life's the punchline, goodness knows!'
As echoes fade into the night,
The search for answers feels just right.

Inquiries on a Slippery Slope

A penguin slipped on ice so slick,
Claiming it's part of his genius trick.
He wobbled, twirled, and gave a shout,
'Is this what life's really all about?'

A walrus chuckled from his rock,
'In questioning, you'll just unlock!'
But while they ponder the cosmic vibe,
The fish are laughing. Oh, what a tribe!

The seals, they juggle with fish in tow,
Wondering where all the answers go.
With bubbles rising in glorious glee,
They know that joy is the true decree!

Amidst the flippers and frolicsome friends,
They realize the search is never end.
For in the laughter, they've found the gold,
With each new slip, a story told.

Melodies from the Abyss

Beneath the waves where mermaids croon,
A crab hums a nonsensical tune.
With seaweed hats and shells in tow,
They disco dance, putting on a show.

An octopus plays a grand guitar,
Singing of dreams that stretch afar.
Tangled tales in the ocean blue,
They inquire if they're ever true.

A dolphin flips high, searching for sense,
While clownfish giggle with innocence.
In the depths, where laughter rings,
The joy of living, the heartstrings sing.

Each note a puzzle, a funny folk,
In the depths of life, they laugh and poke.
With melodies that float and dive,
They savor the journey, oh so alive!

Unwritten Pages of Destiny

With quills in hand, they scribble still,
On pages blank, with comedic thrill.
A cat debates with a wise old rat,
'What's the plot? Or, where's the spat?'

The great white page, an endless sea,
A canvas where the silly run free.
With every scratch, a giggle spills,
As they write down their fanciful thrills.

The dog chimes in with a paw-typed tale,
Of chasing dreams and wagging his tail.
From cozy nooks to raucous plays,
They scrawl their hopes in a playful craze.

So here they sit, with hearts ablaze,
Crafting jokes in myriad ways.
The unwritten path is filled with jest,
For in each scribble lies their quest!

Notes from an Insomnia of Thought

Counting sheep in my head,
They all wear tiny hats,
Bouncing thoughts like bouncy balls,
Did I leave the oven on?

Midnight snacks speak to me,
Crackers with their crispy charms,
Life is but a riddle shown,
Why does my clock tick so loud?

Dreams of pasta twirl and dance,
Oh, is that a flying cow?
Wrestling with a pillow fight,
Perhaps I lost my mind again.

Laughter echoes through the night,
As stars peek in surprise,
Why do we ponder and twirl?
Maybe I'll sleep tomorrow night.

Searching for Stars in Shadows

In the alley where dreams play,
I trip on my own two feet,
Stars keep hiding from my view,
Are they shy or just on strike?

With a flashlight in my pocket,
I aim it at the nearest tree,
Even shadows seem to giggle,
What's their secret? Tell me, please!

Chasing those elusive sparks,
Like cats chasing after tails,
Do the stars get tired, too?
Or just have better things to do?

I grab some friends for the quest,
We dance with shadows, take a bow,
Underneath a moonlit sky,
Laughing at our silliness.

The Enigma of Our Days

Why do socks constantly disappear?
They join a secret sock club,
My coffee tastes like old shoes,
What is life without a little spice?

Toasters always burn my bread,
But perfect pancakes smile back,
Do our kitchens hold a grudge?
Or just waiting for the weekend?

Time rolls on like a great big ball,
Chasing us with no clear aim,
Sometimes it wears a cartoon face,
Mocking us as we ponder why.

We laugh in the face of fate,
While tripping over our own shoes,
Each mishap a comedy show,
Maybe life's just a silly jest.

Lighthouses in the Fog

Drifting through the thickest mist,
Where am I? Space and time,
Lighthouses wink and giggle bright,
Are they flirting or giving hints?

Navigating with a cupcake,
Sprinkles over stars above,
Fog lights swirl like dance-offs,
Is there a prize for best move?

Waves crash like playful puppies,
Splashing my deep thoughts away,
Between the laughs and the sighs,
Do I need a GPS for dreams?

So I'll navigate the unknown,
With a smile and a silly hat,
At the end of this strange path,
Perhaps there's pizza and a cat.

Lights in the Abyss

In the depths where shadows creep,
I trip over thoughts that just won't sleep.
With a wink and a grin, I juggle my woes,
Hoping the answers are hiding in a nose.

The universe laughs as I take a leap,
Falling for wisdom, but it's just a sheep.
I've chased my tail through a cosmic cafe,
Where planets serve coffee in a comical way.

I ask a star if it knows the score,
It twinkles back—just one and no more.
A laugh in the silence, the cosmos stays sly,
Winking its eye as I stumble by.

So here I am, with a smile in tow,
Searching for truth in a cosmic show.
With joy in my heart and a quip on my lips,
I'll dance through the unknown, taking silly trips.

Bridges Between the Known and Unknown

I built a bridge from my couch to the sky,
Waving at clouds as they float on by.
Each step I take, I trip on a dream,
Teetering on thoughts that burst at the seam.

With rubbery legs and a laugh that's bright,
I bounce on the planks of this quirky flight.
The known is fuzzy and the unknown is bold,
Kind of like that story my grandpa once told.

A goosey gander gives me a shout,
"Hey, where are you headed? What's this all about?"
I shrugged and I giggled, "Just taking a peek,
For answers to find, I seek and I seek."

So if you find me there waving at stars,
Just know that I'm lost, but I'm driving fancy cars.
With humor in pocket and joy in my stride,
I'll bridge every gap with a whimsical ride.

Whispers of Existence

In the whispering winds, secrets take flight,
Tickling my eardrums in dead of night.
I ask a leaf for its wisdom and grace,
It chuckles and flutters, saying, "What's your place?"

With each rustle, the cosmos confides,
Giggles through branches where mystery hides.
The moon winks down, a mischievous glow,
As I stumble upon what I don't quite know.

Crickets are chirping a riddle or two,
Their serenade swirling in midnight blue.
I'm turning the pages of what's ever near,
An open book of laughter and cheer.

So listen closely to whispers that fly,
They might just be nuggets from the great big sky.
With quirky questions to add to the blend,
The journey's the joke, and the punchline's my friend.

Echoes of Unanswered Questions

In the hall of echoes, I holler and shout,
As questions bounce back, but find no route.
"Why is the sky blue?" I call with a grin,
An echo just giggles and says, "Try again!"

I'm tossing my thoughts like a salad of fate,
With croutons of wonder piled high on my plate.
The answers keep dodging like cats in the night,
As I chase down my queries with goofy delight.

With every bounce, a new joke unfolds,
A cosmic comedian, or so it is told.
I laugh at my questions as they drift far away,
Finding joy in the hunt, come what may.

So here's to the echoes, the giggles they claim,
For life's not a puzzle but a whimsical game.
With questions aplenty, and answers askew,
I'll dance through the void—just me and my view.

Inquiries in the Garden of Dreams

What if daisies held the key?
To secrets whispered by the bee?
Do gnomes know where the treasure lies?
Or just enjoy the sunny skies?

Is the moon a giant cheese delight?
Or simply shining through the night?
We ask the stars, they giggle loud,
While they dance behind a fluffy cloud.

If worms can squirm and squabble too,
Do they ponder what's the right shoe?
Maybe sandcastles have a view,
Of secrets deep, like morning dew.

Let's toast to dreams both big and small,
To questions that perplex us all!
For in this garden, wild and free,
We plant our doubts, and drink our tea.

Navigating the Labyrinth of Purpose

In a maze of socks and mismatched shoes,
What do we seek? The latest news?
A map of life, or just a snack?
Maybe it's time for a quick nap!

With signs that point to don't go there,
And arrows leading to a bear!
Do ducks conspire with rubber geese?
To find the path of inner peace?

Grasshoppers speak in riddles too,
As they leap from here to who knows where?
Is it the footpath or just a road?
Either way, carry your own load!

We twirl in circles, round and round,
With giggles lost but wisdom found.
Each turn we take, a laugh, a bump,
Navigating life like a silly jump!

Shadows of Eternity

When shadows stretch like silly strings,
Do they dance to unknown flings?
Are ghosts just after that last bite?
Or here to share a late-night fright?

Why do we worry about what's next?
Is life just a giant text?
Do commas lead to coffee chats?
And questions linger like curious cats?

If the sun takes naps, then what about us?
Do we dream in colors or ride on the bus?
With each passing sigh, we giggle and grin,
For shadows remind us to let the fun in!

Eternity's secrets may bring a laugh,
As we chase our tails on this old giraffe.
So let's dance with shadows until we trip,
And find joy in every silly slip!

Dancing with the Unknowable

Inviting mystery to the ball,
We spin and twirl, we jump and crawl!
What's the point? We cannot say,
But let's do the hokey pokey anyway!

With hats made of question marks in tow,
We ask the flowers if they know.
Do trees ponder where they've been?
Or dance with squirrels, a wiggly scene?

Twirling through life's whimsical maze,
We find a rhythm in the crazed.
If living's a riddle, let's choose to laugh,
And dance with the ungraspable half!

The unknown beckons with a wink,
Let's spin through stars and just rethink.
For life's a jest, a playful tease,
And joy is found in wobbly knees!

Beneath Every Breath

In every gasp, a giggle hides,
Questions bounce like ping-pong tides.
Why do we trip on words so sly?
Maybe it's just to wonder why.

We scramble up the ladder of time,
Chasing the clock in rhymes and chimes.
But when we fall, we laugh uproar,
For chaos is just life's encore.

With every hiccup, life's a jest,
Like a squirrel making a peanut quest.
We fumble through our daily plot,
Finding joy in every knot.

So take a breath, let laughter soar,
In this mad dance, there's so much more.
With each new step, let's not defile,
For laughter's the trick, with style and guile.

Journey Through Uncertainty

We boarded a bus with no mapped route,
In search of answers, we giggle and shout.
With a map upside down, we ask, "Where to?"
"Just keep laughing; that's how we get through."

Each bump sends us flying, then crash—ouch!
In this wild ride, we strangely couch.
Questions like confetti, they swirl and fly,
"Is this the exit?" "No, just the sky!"

We stop for snacks, a cosmic delight,
Tacos and twinkies amid starry light.
With no clear destination or guide,
We treasure the snacks more than the ride.

So here's to the chaos; here's to the jest,
Life's a grand trip, so forget the rest.
Let curiosity dance in every mind,
For when we wander, surprises unwind.

Inkblots of Illumination

Doodles on napkins, a scribble parade,
Thoughts splat like paint in a wild cascade.
"What's this?" you ask, as you blink with grace,
It's just life's doodle in a scrambled place.

Worms in bow ties, clouds made of cheese,
Inkblots of questions, but always with ease.
A universe flips in a toddler's grin,
In chaos, my friend, that's where we begin.

Like a giant puzzle lost in the night,
Every piece whispers, "Just stay in flight."
The more we ponder, the more we crash,
Creating new worlds in a wobbly clash.

So raise your pens to each riddle we face,
In the inkblot of life, there's no need for pace.
Let's scribble together, a grand, goofy spree,
For laughter's the color, and wild is the key.

Cartography of the Soul

We're mapping these roads with spaghetti strands,
Where are we going? No one understands.
With maps full of doodles and arrows askew,
"Onward!" we cheer, with a wobbly view.

Each path we take is a loop-de-loop,
Sailing this journey, we're one funky group.
Through valleys of giggles and mountains of fun,
We dance through the shadows, not just in the sun.

Coordinates scribbled on a tissue,
Finding lost treasures, what's your issue?
With compass a-spinning and hearts full of glee,
We wander and wonder, just you and me.

So let's chart this crazy, grand escapade,
In the map of the heart, let laughter cascade.
For every wrong turn leads to joy we find,
In the cartography of souls intertwined.

Colors of the Unfathomable

In a world so vast and bright,
Colors clash with sheer delight.
Red is rubies, green is grass,
Who knew yellow could be so crass?

The blue we wear, a painter's joke,
Splash and swirl, then watch us choke.
Finding rainbows in the mist,
Life's absurdity can't be missed!

Glimmers dance in every hue,
Mixing morals, what's true?
Orange dreams, like silly hats,
Life's a circus with clumsy cats.

So grab a brush and paint the sky,
With every splash, we learn to fly.
In colors bright, we weave our tales,
With giggles loud and gusty gales.

Whispers Between the Stars

Stars do gossip in the night,
Chattering 'bout our wild flight.
They say we dance with flair and style,
And occasionally trip, but just for a while.

Nebulas giggle, planets tease,
With cosmic puns that aim to please.
Asteroids roll their eyes in jest,
At the chaos we call our quest.

Shooting stars just drift and sigh,
'Will they ever learn to fly?'
'Not if they keep forgetting their map!'
They chuckle softly, then take a nap.

In this vastness, we are small,
But laughter echoes, and that's the call.
In every twinkle, secrets blend,
Life's a joke, with no clear end.

In Search of the Unseen Door

Upon a hill, a door appears,
We knock with hope and bounce our cheers.
A squirrel scurries, then gives us a frown,
'What do you seek, in this sleepy town?'

Maps are scribbled, paths entice,
Finding doors is a roll of dice.
'Turn left at the cactus, then right at the bee,'
Said the wise old turtle, sipping his tea.

We twist and turn, then hit a wall,
Oops, wrong door! Let's try that hall.
Maybe the next one opens wide,
With chocolate rivers or a kaleidoscope ride?

Yet every step feels like a song,
With every twist, we can't be wrong.
So here we stand, forever more,
With grins and giggles, in search of the door.

A Compass Beyond the Known

With a compass that spins like a top,
We sail the seas, and occasionally flop.
North is where the laughter lies,
And south is where the silly prize.

East is coffee, the best 'pick-me-up',
While west holds tacos, so fill your cup!
With every direction, a brand new cheer,
Life's little quirks keep drawing us near.

Far away, the horizon blurs,
The compass hums, and off it stirs.
'What's that signal?' we scratch our heads,
Maybe it's just a flock of bread.

In the end, it's all quite fun,
With every twist under the sun.
So let's lose ourselves and roam the map,
After all, life's but one big mishap!

Paradoxes of Perspective

In every mirror, truths collide,
A squirrel might know, but won't confide.
Life's like a pie, absurdly sliced,
Some crumbs are sweet, while others are spiced.

The cat sits smug, in sunlit streams,
While we chase answers, lost in dreams.
Logic dances, wearing a clown's nose,
Is wisdom just weariness in funny clothes?

Is a donut round, or is it just fate?
Answers come late, much like dinner plates.
In a garden of riddles, we often tread,
While chasing the cat, who's long since fled.

So let's laugh at puzzles, take them in stride,
With each twist and turn, let joy be our guide.
For amidst the chaos, wise or not,
It's the quirky journey that can hit the spot.

At the Edge of Understanding

We stand on cliffs of thought pondering,
Where logic ends, and laughs are wandering.
If life's a quiz, what's the right tool?
A rubber chicken or a trip to the pool?

At twilight, shadows play on our backs,
With each lost answer, humor attacks.
The universe chuckles as we take a chance,
On each whacky theory and interstellar dance.

Questions poke fun, like jesters at court,
With wisdom as fleeting as a brief airport.
So let's juggle queries, perhaps juggle some fries,
Life's too absurd for well-structured ties.

In a world full of jest, embrace all the quirks,
For the edge of understanding often just smirks.
When jokes intertwine with philosophical thoughts,
We find the fun in all the tangled knots.

When Questions Bloom

In gardens of queries, questions take flight,
Like daisies in spring, sprouting with delight.
Each petal a ponder, each stem a new chase,
While bees hum the tunes of an odd ballad's grace.

Why are we here? Is it just for a laugh?
To chase after rainbows or wide-eyed giraffes?
With every blunder, we prune and we weed,
Where laughter's the sunlight, that helps us succeed.

As tulips sip tea with the daffodils,
Philosophers mingle 'round with their quills.
They bicker 'bout meanings and tiptoe on lines,
While squirrels in top hats engage in real crimes.

When questions bloom, it's a joyous affair,
Where wisdom's a joke that we all like to share.
Let's plant seeds of laughter and water them well,
For the garden of life holds stories to tell.

Legacies of the Lost

What's left behind in the sands of time?
An old sock's legacy or an un-penned rhyme?
Forgotten are the treasures we fail to collect,
While slip-ups become gems, a curious effect.

In shuffleboard worlds where misfits collide,
Lost thoughts and wild dreams go for a ride.
Like socks without partners, we wander alone,
In mismatched existence, we've made our own zone.

The whispers of past echoes play hide and seek,
In hallways of humor, they giggle and sneak.
From jesters of history, we borrow a cheer,
For each wrinkle and mishap, we hold oh so dear.

So toast to the lost, with crazy delight,
For in every quirk, there's a spark just right.
Embrace their odd legacies, raise up a glass,
For life's greatest treasures may forever elude us.

Patterns in the Wilderness

In the woods where squirrels hide,
Patterns dance with nature's tide.
A tree that leans, a rock that smiles,
Life's odd humor spans the miles.

A rabbit hops, a bird takes flight,
Searching for answers in broad daylight.
But every clue just seems absurd,
Like chiming clocks that never heard.

The wind whispers secrets, quite a tease,
While ants march off like little bees.
They pile their food with great delight,
But seldom find a snack at night.

So out we roam, with laughs and winks,
In search of deep, profound food for thoughts, and links.
Though wisdom seems to play a game,
It's nature's jesters we have to blame.

The Unanswered Call

A phone rings loud, but I ignore,
Who needs the noise? I'll close the door.
With popcorn bowls and comfy seats,
I ponder life through endless feats.

The universe calls, but I'm out chillin',
Laughing at fate with too much fillin'.
When questions linger, I eat a slice,
Life's riddle wrapped up in a cake of rice.

What's the point? I munch and muse,
With chocolate snacks and fuzzy shoes.
The stars may twinkle, but I just sigh,
For deep thoughts deserve a slice of pie.

So if you're lost, just take a break,
Dance in your socks, for goodness' sake!
The answers wander, so let them stall,
Grab a snack instead of the unanswered call.

Soliloquies of Solitude

In a room that's painted blue,
Talking to myself, just us two.
The mirror nods, the clock spins round,
In silent laughs, no wisdom found.

Each snack I munch holds stories rare,
Life's greatest truths? Well, who would care?
I sit and ponder, but it's a hoot,
Wearing socks that don't match, that's the root.

Solitude's song is a quirky tune,
Sung by the fridge at late afternoon.
With every bite of ice cream's bliss,
I cringe and chuckle—what did I miss?

So here's to pondering deep and wide,
With laundry piled up and destiny fried.
In quiet spaces, laughter swirls,
The jokes on us, as life unfurls.

Woven Threads of Wonder

Life's like a sweater with holes galore,
With every tug, it's a little more sore.
Yet, amidst the fray and tangled yarn,
We find our joy where frontiers are worn.

Each thread a dream that's frantically spun,
In the looms of fate where the laughter's begun.
With tangled thoughts and colors bright,
We weave our tales until the night.

So stitch away with needle and glee,
Crafting the tales that set us free.
For though the fabric frays and tears,
The laughter holds us, despite our cares.

With socks on hand and stories to share,
We wander through whims without a care.
As each thread pulls tight, and life's a game,
We laugh through the mess, it's all the same.

Amidst the Chaos of Creation

In a world of swirling dandelions,
Giraffes wear hats and dance with lions.
The sky is blue and the grass is green,
But why's my sock still missing, unseen?

Birds play chess with squirrels in flight,
While ants hold parades through the night.
A bubble wand finds a rainbow arc,
And I ponder snacks while it gets dark.

Life is a puzzle, quite absurd,
Where cats declare it's their turn to herd.
Lost in thought, I munch on pie,
Wondering why my goldfish can't fly.

With giggles and grins, I'll carry on,
My teapot sings of a new dawn.
Amongst the chaos, I raise a toast,
To the strange things I treasure the most.

The Diary of a Wandering Soul

Once I searched for wisdom deep,
But found a frog who couldn't leap.
His croaks were riddles, loud and clear,
As I scribbled thoughts in a can of beer.

I wandered fields of jellybean,
Met a unicorn who was quite mean.
He stomped around, all grumpy and round,
While I giggled at the myths I found.

My heart dripped ink on pages bright,
As I danced with shadows in the moonlight.
But the stars above twinkled with cheer,
Saying, "Don't take life too grave, my dear!"

So here's my tale — a jumbled mess,
Of laughter, quirks, and a little stress.
As I pen these lines of absurdity bold,
Life's just a story waiting to unfold.

Clocks and Constellations

Tick-tock goes the cosmic clock,
As I try to find my missing sock.
Stars wink tales of how time flies,
But here I am, just eating fries.

Calendars flip like pancakes, fast,
Saying ages don't matter, they're just a blast.
A cat named Whiskers keeps perfect time,
While I misplace my thoughts—oh, sublime!

Each second counts, or maybe not,
When I can't decide between tea or a shot.
Constellations form a silly dance,
While I trip and stumble in my pants.

So here's to clocks and starry skies,
To lost keys and forgotten pies.
With laughter rumbled like thunder's roll,
I'll chase the tick-tock of my wandering soul.

Riddles of the Heart

What beats so loud but can hold a tear?
It's like a wild drum with no clear steer.
Is it the pizza from last night's feast?
Or a crush on a dragon? Well, at least!

Cupcakes whisper secrets sweet,
While hearts do a cha-cha in retreat.
With giggles and hiccups, love's a dance,
A tumble-down hill of pure happenstance.

In the riddle of romance, laughter's the key,
Unlocking doors to what could be.
So bring on the sweets, and let's be absurd,
Let's toast to this chaos with a joyous word!

For hearts are like piñatas, bright and spun,
Filled with surprises — we all want fun!
In this playground of feelings from the start,
I'll keep spinning the riddles of the heart.

Sculpting Questions with Time

In a world of clay and rhyme,
I shape my thoughts, one at a time.
With giggles here and snickers there,
My queries dance in the open air.

A sculptor kneads with a playful grin,
As questions twist and do their spin.
Like shadow puppets on a wall,
Do big thoughts really feel so small?

What's cheese without a little mold?
Can a secret be kept when it's bold?
I chuckle loud, then take a seat,
While pondering life's savory treat.

So grab a chisel, let's embark,
On this whimsical journey, join the lark.
With laughter's joy, we sharpen our tools,
As we sculpt away the silly rules.

The Palette of Possibilities

I dip my brush in hues of doubt,
Swirling smiles, what's life about?
A splash of blue, a dash of red,
Mixing joy with thoughts in my head.

Each color swirls, begins to sing,
As goofy questions take to wing.
Is popcorn just a corn's great dream?
And are we more than we might seem?

I paint my canvas, wide and bright,
With strokes of laughter, pure delight.
More purple, please, for quirky quests,
In this art, my heart truly rests.

So here's to canvases yet to come,
With painted hopes and beats of drum.
Each question raised is another coat,
On the palette of my silly boat.

Ascent into the Questions

Up the hill of pondering thoughts,
I hike with glee, amid the plots.
With every step, a query blooms,
Like daisies swaying in cheerful rooms.

Do fish ponder life's messy bait?
Could socks be secretly second-rate?
With every giggle I gain some height,
In this ascent, I feel all right.

With clouds beneath my curious feet,
I ride the breeze, so light and sweet.
Each question lingers, floats on by,
Do butterflies know how to fly?

So up I go, through tickles and sighs,
In the realm where the outlandish lies.
With thoughts like kites, I catch the air,
In this ascent, life's joy is rare.

Navigating the Sea of Doubt

In a boat made of giggles, I drift along,
The waves are questions, a bubble song.
With paddles of laughter, I row with glee,
In the sea of doubt, I'm wild and free.

What if oceans are just puddles, vast?
Could future whales once have been fast?
As each wave crashes with chuckles loud,
I navigate through this wobbly crowd.

Captain Chuckles, that's my name,
In these waters, I play the game.
With jellyfish jokes and starfish yells,
I chart my course where humor dwells.

With a compass of quirk and a map of cheer,
I sail through life and shed every fear.
For in this vast sea, with friends about,
There's joy to be found, no shadow of doubt.

Paths Untraveled

In a world with so many signs,
I chose a path with no defined lines.
My GPS said, 'Turn left at the tree,'
But I ended up in a crabby pet's spree.

Wandered past questions, lost in thought,
Figured wisdom comes from all the things caught.
With snickers and giggles blowing through the air,
The meaning might be hiding under a chair.

Took a shortcut through life's crazy maze,
Where logic twists and everybody plays.
Laughter erupts from every closed door,
In this wild search, who knows what's in store?

Every road less traveled, a giggle or two,
Like finding a sock, that's meant for a shoe.
So here's to adventures we can't fully explain,
With punchlines and puns, let's dance in the rain!

Philosophies Shattered

Sipping tea with Socrates bold,
He spilled the leaves—such wisdom untold!
Tried to juggle reason, but it slipped away,
Now my brain holds a comedy buffet.

Plato sighed, 'What's real?' with a frown,
As I tripped on thoughts while wearing a gown.
Kant suggested I just stick to my street,
But my shoes were mismatched—what a treat!

With every deep thought, I stumbled and fell,
Who needs enlightenment when pizza is swell?
My friends all chuckle while I ponder away,
Perhaps my life's goal is just fun every day!

So here we are, a riddle gone wrong,
In search of the truth, we'll sing a wrong song.
With laughter our guide, and confusion our spark,
Just pass me the punchline—it's time for a lark!

Threads of Infinity

A spaghetti of thoughts, I twirl on a fork,
Noodles of meaning, pasta to gawk.
Saucy ideas slide right off my plate,
As I ponder existence and just want to sate.

An infinite loop like an overcooked riff,
Each twist is bizarre, like a cosmic gift.
Laughter forever woven in the strands,
Who knew finding joy took so many hands?

Perhaps life is simply a tangled-up string,
The more that we pull, the more joy we bring.
So let's dance with kittens, and sing with the breeze,
In this madcap affair, let's do as we please!

In threads of hilarity, we all intertwine,
Questions remain, but we sip on good wine.
So let's break out the jokes, let serendipity thrive,
And keep spinning laughter—now that's being alive!

Reflections in a Cracked Mirror

Glancing at me, a fun-house surprise,
A circus of chuckles and mismatched eyes.
With all my quirks, I grin at my face,
Waving back at the chaos, sheer interface.

In shattered glass, wisdom's hard to find,
But the jokes that we tell are always aligned.
My reflection is puzzled, lost in a haze,
Yet he leans toward laughter in so many ways.

I dabble in questions that bounce off the wall,
'Is my hair out of place? Should I stand up tall?'
But in this weird realm, I find my delight,
With each crack reflecting a silly insight.

So let's toast to the odd and bizarre,
A life full of humor, spread near and far.
With mirrors and laughter, let's dance in the glow,
And cherish the chaos wherever we go!

Unraveling the Fabric of Being

In a world of socks that do not match,
I ponder why we start to scratch.
Is it in purpose or simply a game,
Or are we just puppets, all the same?

Are we lost in the forest or merely blind?
Or hunting for treasures that we can't find?
With a pizza slice for a polished soul,
Are we seeking meaning or just a nice roll?

Do we chase the rainbows or play in the mud?
Does it matter if we end up in a flood?
With clues like breadcrumbs leading us on,
Are we just here till the pizza is gone?

So I'll laugh at the stars as they spin and twirl,
And dance with my doubts in this quirky whirl.
With each twist and turn, I'll embrace the fun,
For the joy is the journey, and we're not yet done.

Questions in the Silence

In the stillness where thoughts like to roam,
I wonder if chaos might lead me home.
Is life a riddle wrapped in a jest,
Or just a long nap where we're all guests?

Do fish dream of water while swimming around?
Is laughter just noise that's lost in the sound?
With questions like bubbles that pop and then burst,
I giggle at answers that always come first.

Is my cat truly plotting to take over space?
Does my goldfish wonder about its own grace?
With wisdom like crumbs falling under my chair,
Are we all just players in a silly affair?

So I'll toast to the questions that tickle my mind,
That jiggle my thoughts and leave reason behind.
As I ponder the cosmos with a cup of tea,
I'm thankful for questions that don't set me free.

Footprints on the Path of Wonder

With footprints left in the sand of my dreams,
I trudge through life on a path full of memes.
Some folks say it's serious, a solemn old game,
But I'm here to giggle and play without shame.

With a wink at the universe, I step and I sway,
And gather my questions like kids at a play.
Are we the punchline, the joke of it all?
Or just spectral whispers, upon their grand call?

Did the chicken cross to find wisdom and peace?
Or was it just tired of munching on cheese?
With laughter like confetti, I take in the sight,
Every step on this path feels shockingly bright.

So I'll dance with my shadows, embrace the unknown,
With joy in my heart, I'll never feel alone.
For every twirl and stumble brings forth a new chance,
To skip through this life in a totally weird dance.

Fragments of a Fleeting Moment

In this fleeting moment, I spot a lost sock,
Is life just a puzzle or a ticking clock?
With snippets of sunshine and clouds made of cheese,
I savor odd moments that bring me to tease.

Are we sketching our stories with crayons and quirks?
Or trapped in the hamster wheel, doing our works?
With laughter like bubbles that float and then pop,
Do we chase after meaning or just take a swap?

With a wink at the chaos that fills every day,
I gather my giggles and send them on their way.
Is the gap 'tween our eyebrows the answer we seek?
Or a ticklish thought that just makes us feel weak?

So let's paint with the colors that spill from our hearts,
And dance with the questions that life imparts.
For in each fleeting moment, we find joy in the jest,
And laugh at the wonders that we love the best.

Explorations at the Edge of Thought

I wandered through a field of dreams,
Where questions float like silly beams.
A chicken crossed with utmost glee,
To ponder why it crossed at three.

With magnifying glass and a grin,
I searched for wisdom tucked within.
Found a sock, half a sandwich too,
Sometimes, life's puzzles are just askew.

A squirrel debated life's great lore,
While searching desperately for more.
He said, 'If I just had a nut,
I'd solve the mystery, who knows what!'

Every thought a little prankster,
Twisting truths, an unexpected dancer.
Yet laughter bubbles in the maze,
As minds collide in a comedic haze.

Tides of Meaning in Shifting Sands

On a beach where thoughts collide,
I wrote my dreams, the tide my guide.
Waves laughed loud, they swirled and spun,
    Claiming wisdom's just a pun.

Seagulls squawked at philosophic chats,
    Debating life with chittering rats.
    A crab joined in, a sage, no less,
Said, 'Just be cool, don't overstress!'

Shells held secrets, whispered light,
    In the shadows of day and night.
I filled my bucket with jests and quirks,
    Finding joy in the strange works.

    Mirth and chaos hand in hand,
    Life's absurdity, a silly band.
    So let's dance along this shore,
With laughter echoing forevermore.

Labors of the Inquisitive Soul

I toiled in the garden of thought,
Picking flowers that time forgot.
The weeds of doubt grew tall and wide,
But curiosity was my guide.

An odd beetle spoke in rhyme,
'Life's just a joke with no set time.'
I asked him how to find the truth,
He blinked and said, 'Just be uncouth!'

With a shovel made of laughter's sheen,
I dug for answers, yet unseen.
Found a mirror, cracked but bold,
Reflections of stories yet untold.

Each stumble led to quirky sights,
Why wonder's dance brings such delights.
With every question, joy erupts,
Life's labor's sweet, as laughter corrupts.

Serendipitous Discoveries

In my attic, I found a clue,
An ancient hat, thought it was new.
Wore it proudly, danced a jig,
Only to trip on my old bigwig.

A map led to the fridge, how quaint,
Where pickles waited, a vivid saint.
Each jar a mystery wrapped in brine,
They whispered secrets, 'Life's divine!'

Explored the couch, a treasure trove,
With crumbs of wisdom I can't remove.
A remote, a sock, and a wild old boot,
Sometimes gems hide where life seems mute.

So here's to finding joy in junk,
To every mishap, a grateful funk.
With laughter as our guiding light,
We'll sail through days, playful and bright.

Musings on a Celestial Journey

Up there among the stars so bright,
   I ponder why I left the light.
My coffee's cold, my socks don't pair,
   Yet here I sit, without a care.

A comet zips, it waves and flies,
It guides my thoughts, no need for ties.
   Is life a game or cosmic jest?
Oh, what's for lunch? I just can't guess!

In black holes, secrets might reside,
   But I just want some pizza pie.
   The universe expands so fast,
While I'm still stuck with laundry tasks!

My spaceship's parked—oh, what a sight!
   With candy wrappers, left and right.
   Still seeking truths in all this space,
   I'll need more chips to win this race!

Chronicles of the Unseen

In shadows where the echoes play,
I wonder if I'll find my way.
Invisible threads weave and twine,
I trip and fall—are these all mine?

A ghostly cat with mighty paws,
Is wandering 'round with secret flaws.
Does the fridge hum a heartfelt tune,
Or just complain of late nights, too soon?

The rain drips down like thoughts unaware,
While socks go missing, oh despair!
The candy jar—now holds no more,
Just empty hopes and a missing score.

So here I sit, a funny plight,
In a universe that's not quite right.
I'll take some laughs, a quirky sign,
And maybe then, the stars align!

Beneath the Surface of Everyday

Beneath the bustle, laughs reside,
In daily woes, what do we hide?
A burp, a sneeze, a clumsy feat,
Life's little quirks can't be beat!

The toaster pops, with bread in flight,
Breakfast dreams of flaky delight.
Yet, what is life if crumbs remain,
But joy in chaos? Isn't that insane?

I juggle plans like oranges bright,
And trip on thoughts, a silly sight.
Each coffee spill is a chance to cheer,
A fluffy mess to hold most dear.

So let's embrace the silly grind,
For laughter's gold, and truth we find.
Dance in the rain, laugh with delight,
While life winks back, a grand ol' sight!

Clues in the Chaos

Amidst the clutter and the craze,
Life throws puzzles, in many ways.
A sock-shaped riddle, lost in time,
Or is it just a laundry crime?

The neighbor's dog, a wise old seer,
Barks cryptic clues, but what's the leer?
Is barking wisdom from afar,
Or just a shout for the old car?

I chase my thoughts like butterflies,
In swirling winds, beneath blue skies.
Perhaps the answers come in quirks,
Like how a cat just trills and lurks.

So join me in this nutsy game,
Where questions live and thoughts take aim.
With laughter loud, and hearts so free,
We'll solve the puzzles—just you and me!

Maps of the Heart

In the treasure chest of dreams, we roam,
Searching for love like a dog seeks a bone.
X marks the spot, oh how we contort,
Lost in the maze of our own silly thoughts.

Hand-drawn doodles, arrows that point,
To places unknown, where hearts dare to joint.
With compasses spinning, we laugh and we cry,
Finding our way while we fly oh so high.

A GPS fails when feelings arise,
Only the heart knows where the true path lies.
So we wander, explore, and embrace the bizarre,
In this crazy map, we're each a bright star.

So grab your crayons, let's sketch our delight,
Navigating the quirkiness, day into night.
It's a crooked journey but join in the fun,
With maps of the heart, our lives are well done.

Voices in the Void

Echoes of laughter in the empty space,
Asking big questions, just look at my face.
Is there a meaning, or just a big game?
Whispers of nonsense, oh, who's to blame?

In the cosmic joke, we all play a part,
Conversations with shadows, they tug at your heart.
Hey there, Einstein, care to chime in?
Debating with silence is where we begin.

The void is a canvas, blank and wide,
Painting our thoughts with colors inside.
Like comedians on a stage with no floor,
We search for the punchline, then ask for more.

So let's raise our voices, make some noise,
The void has no limits, just playful joys.
With each witty banter, we make our own choice,
In a world full of questions, let's rejoice!

Gazing into the Infinite

Stars in the night seem to giggle and wink,
As we ponder the universe, on the edge of our brink.
What lies out there in the vast, dark expanse?
Aliens dancing, perhaps, in a cosmic dance?

Peering through telescopes, hoping for proof,
Of life on Mars or a Jovian goof.
"Beam me up, Scotty!" light-hearted requests,
Exploring the cosmos, with our space suits that jest.

Time rips and bends, like a rubbery stretch,
With laughter and wonder, we happily fetch.
In infinite realms, we giggle and spin,
Exploring the absurd, let the giggles begin!

So gaze into stars, let your mind take flight,
In the comedy of cosmos, everything feels right.
With each twinkling star, we're reminded to see,
The infinite laughter in life's mystery.

The Art of Unsung Questions

What's up with socks? They vanish in pairs,
Lost in the dryer while nobody cares.
Why does the cookie crumble off the plate?
Perhaps it's rebel thinking, refusing its fate.

Is the chicken a traveler, bold and young?
Crossing the road for some tunes to be sung?
Each question a riddle, a puzzle we find,
Creating a world where we're joyfully blind.

Why do we trip when we're lost deep in thought?
Bumping into wisdom that can't be bought.
The art of the question, so crafty and sly,
Turns serious matters to laughs in the sky.

So here's to the questions we giggle to ask,
Wrapping wisdom in humor, a merry mask.
In this artistic dance of each quirky quest,
We'll laugh through the puzzle, it's therapy best!

www.ingramcontent.com/pod-product-compliance
Lightning Source LLC
Chambersburg PA
CBHW051634160426
43209CB00004B/636